THE ESSENTIAL HANDBOOK TO DIABETIC INSTANT POT COOKING

TIPS AND RECIPES TO MAKE HEALTHY, DELICIOUS LOW SUGAR AND SUGAR FREE MEALS IN YOUR PRESSURE COOKER

BY

EVELYN CARMICHAEL

Copyright © 2017

Evelyn Carmichael

INTRODUCTION

Instant Pots and Pressure Cookers are very popular kitchen devices these days. And why not? They can reduce your cooking time by half! One kitchen gadget can do the job of 5 other appliances by boiling, sautéing, baking, and cooking your food in one nifty device. Making good choices for your food intake is especially important if you are Prediabetic or Diabetic. The Instant Pot can be a time saver as you are undoubtedly eating more at home to try to control your blood sugar and ensure your body has proper nutrition. This book will give you some delicious recipes to try- all with pictures- and some ideas and tips on how you can use your Instant Pot.

.

Note: cover photos include recipes contained in this book 1. Mexican-style Stuffed Peppers (Vegetarian and Side Dish Chapter), 2. Spaghetti Squash and tomatoes (Vegetarian and Side Dish Chapter), 3. Chicken Stroganoff (Chicken Dishes Chapter), 4. Blueberry Bundt Cake (Dessert chapter).

Evelyn Carmichael

The Essential Handbook to
Diabetic Instant Pot Cooking

TABLE OF CONTENTS

Evelyn Carmichael

LEGAL NOTES

Evelyn Carmichael

CHAPTER 1. THE ADVANTAGES OF COOKING WITH AN INSTANT POT

Pressure cookers can be found in many homes across the country. While many people are discovering this form of cooking for the very first time, pressure cookers have in fact been around for years. My mother, and her mother all had a pressure cooker, using it to create some tasty meals, that we could all enjoy.

The beauty of pressure cookers is that they can cook meals in half the time it usually takes an oven to do the same job. This means that you can literally load the pot up with ingredients, and get on with something else. These days we have what my mother would call a "New-fangled" pressure cooker, which is also known as the 'Instant Pot'. This impressive device doesn't just pressure cook meals, it can steam and slow cook meals too, making it an ideal gadget to have in the kitchen.

Ideal for diabetics

If you have diabetes, you will be pleased to know that the Instant Pot can help you to create delicious, low carb dishes in no time. This potentially means that you will no longer be snacking on sugar-filled foods as you wait for your meal to cook. This wonderful gadget can cook your meals approximately 70% quicker than if they were cooked in the oven. This means that in less than half the time, you could have something delicious to enjoy, without it negatively affecting your sugar level.

The world is your oyster...so to speak

When it comes to creating tasty dishes, the world is your oyster, thanks to the flexibility of the Instant Pot. I know that creating meals when dealing with diabetes can feel quite restrictive, and it's all too tempting to just eat anything you want, and deal with the consequences later. I struggled with Prediabetes and looked for some time for recipes to cut down my sugar intake. After a friend purchased an Instant Pot when they first hit the market, she was more than happy to show me how great it was. Because she decided to slow cook, and pressure cook most of her meals from then on, she was able to control what she ate, and within the space of a few months, my friend and her husband lost 30 pounds between them. This is when I decided to give the Instant Pot a try, and I started using it to control my blood sugar levels, and lose a bit of weight too. The beauty of this gadget is that you can pretty much cook anything in it, which means you have the chance to reduce the impact diabetes has on your life, while also enjoying tasty and nutritious foods.

Why Should You Cook With An Instant Pot?

We know that we're supposed to eat a healthy balanced diet, that is low in carbs, but high in foods that will maintain our sugar levels so it doesn't get too high, and it doesn't fall. The trouble is that we don't always eat as well as we should, simply because cooking nutritious meals can take a lot of time. The good news is that every recipe that you'll find in this book will help you out. They will make mealtimes so much easier, and they will benefit you from a health perspective too.

If you have diabetes, you will know that you should ideally eat foods that contain a lot of fiber, and slow-releasing sugar. The recipes contained in this book all fit into those criteria, but you know your body better than anyone. If there is something in a recipe that you know doesn't agree with your blood sugar levels, feel free to swap it out.

Instant Pot or Regular Oven?

Let's now take a closer look at how the Instant Pot can prove to be better than using an oven. Many of us have used our ovens for years, as a way to cook a wide variety of meals. While there is absolutely nothing wrong with cooking this way, it can take a lot of time to create dishes for the family, or even just for yourself.

When it comes to using your Instant Pot, your meals will be ready in less than half the time, and you won't have to limit what you cook. For example, an oven will cook whatever you place in it, but all it will do is cook the food. An Instant Pot will steam, slow cook, or pressure cook your meals. It can also do other things too, making it an incredibly useful thing to have in your home.

You may love cooking just as much as I do, but after a long hard day, you might not always feel like spending hours in the kitchen. This is where the Instant Pot can come in and help you. You can prepare delicious and healthy meals that will not badly impact your sugar levels, and you can do all of this in less than half the time.

The Essential Handbook to
Diabetic Instant Pot Cooking

Evelyn Carmichael

CHAPTER 2. SIDE AND VEGETARIAN DISHES

Garlic infused Corn on the cob

Ingredients:

2 ears of corn
2 cups of water
1 clove of garlic
2 TBS butter

Method

Place the steamer basket in your Instant Pot, and add a cup of water in there. Now place the garlic and corn in the basket, and close the lid. Cook on high for 2 minutes, and release the pressure quickly. Remove the corn from the Pot, and serve. Note: to make an extra garlic corn on the cob, retrieve steamed garlic clove and mix with butter. Spread on corn.

Goat cheese risotto with zucchini

Serves 3
Ingredients:

1 garlic clove (Minced)
1/3 cup of onion (sliced)
1 TBS of lemon juice
½ cup zucchini (sliced)
¼ chopped tomatoes
1 ½ cups of vegetable broth
1 TBS of olive oil
¼ cup of toasted pecans (sliced)
2 ounces of goat cheese (Soft)
3/4 cup of Arborio rice
Black pepper
¼ cup of white wine
1 pound shrimp (cooked, peeled and deveined)
(optional) to make this an entree

Method

Pour the olive oil into the Pot and 'Sauté' until the oil has started to heat up. Add the onions and garlic, and stir for about 5 minutes, or until the onion is soft. Now add the rice, and stir again. Cook for 1 minute, and add the wine, and stir. Allow the wine to be absorbed, and then add the broth and zucchini, stir, and select 'High'. As soon as the pressure is high, lower the heat to medium and cook for 5 minutes. Lower the pressure quickly, and add the shrimp and tomatoes. Stir, and cook for 2-3 minutes with the lid off. Stir, add the lemon juice and pepper, and stir. Now add the cheese, mix well, and serve with the pecans sprinkled on top.

Note: I often substitute whatever I have on hand for this dish. Zucchini not in season? Spinach or butternut squash works wonderfully.

Mexican-style stuffed peppers

Serves 2
Ingredients:

½ pound of turkey (Ground)
2 slices Jack pepper cheese
2 bell peppers (seeds removed, top & innards
removed)
2 ounces of green chilies (sliced)
½ tsp of salt
1 green onion (sliced)
½ tsp of garlic powder
½ jalapeno (seeds removed, sliced)
½ tsp of cumin
¼ cup of bread crumbs
1 tsp of chili powder (Ground)
¾ cup of sour cream
pinch of garlic powder
½ TBS of chipotle sauce

Juice of ½ lime
Zest of ½ lime
½ cup of water

Method

Add the chipotle sauce, zest, juice, and cream to a bow, and mix well. Add the garlic powder, and mix again. Set to one side. In another bowl, add the rest of the ingredients apart from the peppers, and cheese and mix well. Spoon this mixture into the peppers, ensuring the mix is equally divided between them.

Now add some water to the Pot, and then add the steam rack. Place the peppers on the rack and cook them for 15 minutes on 'High'. Once 15 minutes is up, release the pressure for 10 minutes, and then quickly release any remaining pressure.

Now turn your broiler on, and add the peppers. Add the cheese on top of the peppers, and allow it to brown slightly. Remove the peppers from the broiler, place on plates, and serve.

Note: I often add some black beans and fire roasted corn to this recipe and top with a dollop of sour cream.

Wholegrain basmati rice

Serves 4
Ingredients:

1 ½ cups of wholegrain basmati rice
¾ teaspoon of salt
1 TBS of olive oil
2 ¼ cups of water

Method

Add all of the ingredients to the Pot, and select
'Multigrain'. Allow to cook, and once cooking is done,
leave the lid on for 4-5 minutes, then using a fork,
fluff the rice up, and serve.

Spaghetti squash & tomatoes

Serves 2-3
Ingredients:

1 ½ pounds of spaghetti squash
Salt & pepper
¾ cup of water
½ TBS of olive oil
Pinch of black pepper
1 tsp of salt
½ clove garlic (Minced)
1 TBS of olive oil
1 pint of cherry tomatoes (Halved)

Basil for garnish
1 TBS Parmesan cheese

Method

Place the squash in the Pot, and pour the water in.

Cook on 'High' for 10 minutes, and take the squash out. Cut it in half, and using a spoon, remove the seeds. Now take a fork, and scrape away the pulp, and set it to one side. Squash will resemble "spaghetti" strands.

Add the tomatoes to a strainer and cover them with the salt, and stir. Set to one side for 10-15 minutes. Now pour out the water that's in your Pot, and select 'Sauté' Add the oil, and as soon as it has started to get warm, add the garlic. Cook for about 2 minutes, and then add the squash. Stir well, and add the tomatoes, and stir again. After a few minutes, remove the tomatoes and squash from the Pot, and add divide between plates. Serve with Basil and Parmesan Cheese.

Refried beans

Serves 1
Ingredients:

½ cup of pinto beans (rinsed)
1/8 cup of avocado oil
1 small bay leaf
1 garlic clove (sliced)
1 ½ cups of water
½ jalapeno pepper(Minced)
½ onion (sliced)
½ tsp of salt

Method

Add the beans, water, garlic and bay leaf to the pot, and select 'beans/chili'. Cook for 35 minutes, and then naturally release the pressure. Remove the beans and water, and set to one side. Now press 'Sauté', and add the pepper, onion, and oil, and sauté for 2-3 minutes. Sprinkle the salt on top, stir, and add the beans and water back in there. Now mash the beans and stir them in well. Cook on 'High' for about 5 minutes, or until the bean mixture is thick. Serve.

Lima bean and tomato salad

Serves 2
Ingredients:

½ pound of lima beans (Shelled)
½ pound of kidney, navy, or black bean
1/8 cup of olive oil
1 ½ tomatoes (Peeled, minced)
½ tsp of salt
1 ½ onions (Minced)
¼ cup of white wine vinegar
½ cherry pepper (sliced)
Juice of 1 lime
1 ½ garlic cloves (Minced)
1 TBS of parsley (sliced)
1 green bell peppers (Minced)

2 green onions (sliced)

Method

Add the beans to the Pot, and add enough water so they are covered. Cook on 'High' for 5 minutes, or until the beans are starting to turn soft. Now pour the water out, and allow the beans to cool. Place the remaining ingredients in a bowl, and mix well. Add 1 TBS of water to the bowl, and stir. Now place the beans in a different bowl, and pour the sauce over the top. Serve.

Evelyn Carmichael

CHAPTER 3. SOUPS AND STEWS

These tasty soups and stews dishes that are low in carbs, high in taste, and ideal for those times you need something a little comforting.

Mexican-style Beef Stew

Serves 2-3
Ingredients

1 ¼ pounds beef chuck roast (Cubed)
Pinch black pepper
½ TBS chili powder
¼ tsp fish sauce
¾ tsp salt
¼ cup gluten-free bone broth

1 TBS ghee (ok to substitute butter)
¼ cup tomato salsa
1 onion (Sliced)
½ TBS tomato paste
3 cloves garlic (Crushed)
¼ cup green onion (chopped) OR jalapenos (sliced in rings)

Method:

Add the chili powder, beef, and salt to a bowl and mix well. Now press 'Sauté' on your Instant Pot and once it's hot add the ghee. Allow to melt then add the onions. Cook the onions until they are clear and then add the garlic and tomato paste. Cook for 20-30 seconds. Now add the beef and stir. Add the fish sauce, stock, and salsa. Mix well. Place the lid on the pot and press 'Meat'. Cook for 35 minutes. Once the cooking time is up, release the pressure naturally, and then season the stew also adding in the green onions or jalapenos. Serve.

Note: I often add corn or potatoes to this dish as well as garnish with avocados and a dollop of sour cream.

Chicken stew with corn meal dumplings

Serves 1-2
Ingredients:

1 carrot (sliced)
½ TBS of whole wheat flour
½ celery stalk (sliced)
¼ cup of milk
Small handful corn kernels
¼ tsp of rosemary

½ cup of chicken broth
¼ onion (sliced)
1 chicken thigh (Skinned)
Pinch black pepper
1 garlic clove (Minced)

Dumplings-
1 ¾ cornmeal muffin mix
¼ cup heavy cream
¾ cup milk
¼ cup cheddar cheese
2 TBS green onion

Method

Add the corn, carrots, garlic, onion, pepper, rosemary and celery to the Pot, and add the chicken on top. Now add the broth, and cook on "manual" setting for 14 minutes (fresh chicken) or 20 minutes (frozen chicken). Once the required cooking time is up, quick release the steam and remove the chicken, discarding the bones. Cut the chicken into chunks, and add it back to the Pot.

Mix all dumpling ingredients together and shape into round balls. Add to boiling mixture with lid off and cook for another 10-15 minutes, or until it's cooked to your satisfaction. Season with salt and pepper and Serve.

Pea and ham soup

Serves 4
Ingredients:

8 ounces split peas (Rinsed)
3 ½ cups of water
½ cup of carrots (sliced)
2 ½ ounces of turkey ham
½ onion (sliced)
2 small bay leaves
2 chicken bouillon cubes
1 TBS olive oil

Method
Add oil to sauté pan. Add onion and sauté for 3
minutes. Stir in rest of ingredients to your Pot, and
place lid on Pot. Set to "soup" function and cook for
12 minutes. Let the pressure naturally release. Serve.

Lentil and vegetable soup

Serves 4-5
Ingredients:

1/8 cup of soy protein
3 cups of water
1/3 cup of lentils (Dried)
1/8 cup tomato sauce
¼ cup of onion (sliced)
1 beef bouillon cube
½ cup zucchini (sliced)
½ garlic clove
1 small potato (sliced)
1 basil leaf
½ cup of carrots (sliced)
Pinch black pepper
¼ cup of green beans
½ tsp salt
¼ cup of tomatoes (sliced)

Method

Add all the vegetables to your Pot, and stir well. Now add the spices, lentils, soy, and bouillon cube, and stir again. Add enough water so that the ingredients are just covered. Cook on 'High' until steam starts to come out of the Pot, then lower the pressure to medium/low, and cook for 10-15 minutes. Let the pressure reduce naturally, and serve.

Butternut Squash Soup

Serves 2-3
Ingredients

2 cups butternut squash (Peeled, de-seeded, chopped)
1 tsp tarragon
2 cups sweet potatoes (Peeled, cubed)
½ tsp nutmeg
3 cups gluten-free vegetable broth
1 tsp cinnamon
1 onion (Chopped)
½ tsp turmeric
1 inch of ginger (Peeled)
1 ½ tsp curry powder
2 garlic cloves (Crushed)
1 tsp salt

2 TBS coconut oil

Method:

Press 'Sauté' on the top, and as soon as it's hot, add the salt, ginger, coconut oil, garlic, and onion, and sauté until the onion is a little soft. Add the remaining ingredients and stir well. Select 'Manual', making sure the vent is closed and set the timer for 10 minutes. Once 10 minutes is up, release the pressure naturally, add the soup to a food processor, and blend until it's smooth. Serve.

Chicken and Lentil Soup

Serves 4-5
Ingredients

2 cups lentils (Uncooked)
¼ tsp salt
1 ½ chicken thighs (Boneless, trimmed)
¼ tsp paprika
3 ½ cups water
Pinch oregano
1 TBS bouillon
½ tsp cumin
½ onion (Chopped)
½ tsp garlic powder
1 scallion (Chopped)
½ tomato (Chopped)
1/8 cup cilantro
1 ½ garlic cloves (Chopped)

Method:

Add all of the ingredients to your Instant Pot and stir well. Select 'Soup' and cook for 30 minutes. Once 30 minutes is up, allow the pressure to release and remove the chicken from the pot. Shred the chicken using 2 forks and place it back into the pot. Stir well and serve.

Evelyn Carmichael

CHAPTER 4. CHICKEN DISHES

Chicken Adobo

Serves 3-4
Ingredients

2 pounds chicken
2 green onions (Chopped)
1 TBS olive oil
¼ cup soy sauce
4 bay leaves (Dried)
½ cup soy sauce (Light)
1 red chili (Dried)

¼ cup vinegar
1 tsp black pepper (Ground)
1 TBS fish sauce
1 onion (Minced)
1 TBS sugar substitute (Splenda or Truvia)
8-10 garlic cloves (Crushed)

Method:

Add the soy sauces, fish sauce, sugar, and vinegar to a bowl and mix well. Set to one side. Now pour the oil into the pot and add the chicken, and cook for about 2 minutes, or until it's browned, and then remove it from the pot, and set to one side. Now press 'Sauté' and once the pot is hot, add the onion and garlic and cook for a few minutes. When soft add the bay leaves, pepper, and chili. Sauté for about 30 seconds.

Now add the bowl of sauce mix and stir, de-glazing the pot as you do. Cook on 'High' for 9 minutes before releasing the pressure naturally. Remove the chicken from the pot, place on a plate, sprinkle the onions on top and serve.

Chicken and Rice

Serves: 2-3
Ingredients:

¼ pound of mushrooms (Sliced)
1 cup broccolini
1/3 cup of uncooked rice
¼ cup onion (sliced)
1 cup of water
1 pound chicken pieces (Skinned)
Pinch of salt
½ tsp of chicken bouillon
½ tsp of chicken seasoning

Method

Add the chicken, onion, broccolini, and mushrooms to the Pot, and press 'Sauté'. Cook for about 8-10 minutes, or until the chicken is browned. Add the rest of the ingredients and stir. Place lid on pot and seal pressure vent. Press the rice setting (or "low") for 12 minutes. Quick release pressure and serve.

Chicken Stroganoff

Serves 2-3
Ingredients:

1 pound chicken breasts
½ packet of dry onion mix
½ can of cream of mushroom soup
8 ounces of sour cream
¼ cup fresh mushrooms (sliced)
1 cup egg noodles

Method

Add 1 cup of water to Pot. Cook noodles on high steam for 5 minutes. Set aside.

Add the cream, soup, and onion mix to a bowl, and mix well. Set aside.

Now add the chicken to the Pot, and sauté for 10-12 minutes until brown. Add the mushrooms halfway (at about 5 minutes). Pour the soup mix over the chicken. Sautee until bubbly. Add cooked noodles and continue to sauté for 1 more minute.

Note: To skip a step with the noodles, you can cook them when you add the sauce back to the chicken. Just close the lid and steam for 5 minutes on medium. If you do this method, make sure you don't cook your chicken too long.

Chicken and Mexican cheese

Serves 2-3
Ingredients:

1 pound of chicken breast
½ cup chicken broth
¼ cup of milk
½ can cream of mushroom soup
½ cup Mexican shredded cheese
½ can cheese soup
1 box of whole wheat penne
Taco seasoning mix
Green onion, garnish
Red pepper flakes, garnish

Method

Add the chicken, broth, and taco mix to the Pot. Seal
valve and cook on "chicken" setting. Add 5 minutes to

the cook time for total of 20 so you can quick release the pressure when finished. Remove chicken and shred chicken with two forks. Return to pot.
In a bowl, add the milk, and mushroom and cheese soups, and mix well. Pour this mixture over the chicken and add pasta. Steam on low for 6 minutes. Sprinkle with shredded cheese. Garnish with green onion and red pepper and serve.

The Essential Handbook to
Diabetic Instant Pot Cooking

Evelyn Carmichael

CHAPTER 5. BEEF AND PORK

<u>Mexican style Pulled Pork Lettuce Cups</u>

Serves 2-3
Ingredients:

1 pound of pork roast (Sliced)
Water
½ TBS of olive oil
½ lime (In wedges)
¼ head of butter lettuce
½ carrot (Grated)
¼ TBS of cocoa powder (Unsweetened)
¼ onion (sliced)
¼ tsp of salt
Pinch of cayenne pepper
¼ tsp of red pepper flakes
Pinch of coriander

½ tsp of oregano
¼ tsp of cumin
¼ tsp of white pepper
¼ tsp of garlic powder

Method:

Add the salt, cayenne pepper, red pepper flakes, coriander, oregano, cumin, white pepper, and garlic powder to a bowl, and mix them together well. Set to one side. Now add the onion and the spice mix into the pork, and wrap it up in some baking paper. Add to your refrigerator, and allow to chill for at least 5 hours.

Add the pork to the Pot, and select 'Sauté', and brown on all sides. Once the pork is browned select 'High', and cook for 40-50 minutes. Release the pressure naturally, and take the meat out, and shred it. Set to one side. Spoon the fat out of the Pot, and then add the pork back into the Pot.

Take the lettuce leaves and place them on a plate so they form cup shapes. Sprinkle some carrot on top, and fill the cups with pork. Serve.

Note: You can substitute the meat and vegetables in this recipe to what you have on hand.

Beef Stroganoff

Serves 3-4
Ingredients:

1 pound of beef round steak (Cubed)
1 ½ TBS of olive oil
¼ cup of flour
¼ tsp of salt
½ TBS of Worcestershire sauce
Pinch of pepper
½ medium onion (sliced)
½ can of beef broth
1 cup of mushrooms (sliced)
1 ½ garlic cloves (Minced)
½ cup of sour cream

Evelyn Carmichael

Method

Coat the beef in half the flour, and then add to a skillet, and brown on all sides. Once browned, add the beef to the Instant Pot. Add the garlic and onion to the skillet, and sauté, and then add them to the Pot too.

Now add the rest of the ingredients to the Pot, apart from the flour, and sour cream, and cook on medium/high for 20 minutes, and allow the pressure to naturally release.

Take the rest of the flour, and make a paste with it, and then add it to the broth, and stir. Add the sour cream, and stir well. Serve with rice.

Chinese-style Pork Ribs

Serves 2-3
Ingredients

2 ½ pounds pork spare ribs
½ cup green onions (Chopped)
2 tsp brown sugar substitute (Splenda) or Agave
1 tsp chili and garlic sauce
1 TBS sesame oil
¼ cup garlic (Chopped)
1 ½ TBS soy sauce
3 TBS black beans (Fermented)
1 ½ TBS sherry (Dry)
2 tsp corn starch
1 tsp black pepper

1 ½ tsp salt
1 cup water

Method:

Add all of the ingredients apart from the spare ribs, water, and corn starch to a bowl and mix well. Add the spare ribs, and make sure they are coated in the sauce. Marinade at room temperature for at least 30 minutes. Add the corn starch, and stir well. Now pour the water in your Instant Pot and add the spare ribs and sauce. Press 'High' and cook for 15 minutes, then naturally release the pressure. Serve.

The Essential Handbook to
Diabetic Instant Pot Cooking

Evelyn Carmichael

CHAPTER 6. DESSERT RECIPES

Raspberry Walnut Brownies

Serves 12
Ingredients

1 Box Sugar Free Brownie Mix
½ cup raspberries (smashed)
¼ cup Walnuts (chopped)
1 oz white chocolate (Shaved)
1 cup water

Method:

In bowl, make brownie mix as directed. Add walnuts and smashed raspberries. Pour mixture into a prepared glass baking dish that will fit into your instant pot (generally 8x8 fits well). Add water into reservoir and place dish on steam rack. Add tin foil (tented) to prevent too much moisture on brownie and put lid on machine. Cook on 'Manual' for 35 minutes with pressure valve sealed. Quick release the pressure. Cool and then cut into 12 squares. Add shaved white chocolate to top and serve.

Cranberry Compote

Ingredients:
Makes: 2 cups

10 oz fresh or frozen cranberries
1 apple (peeled, cored, and chopped) (Optional)
½ cup honey
¼ cup lemon juice
1 tsp cinnamon
¼ tsp salt

Method:

Add all ingredients to the Instant Pot and stir. Cook (manual) on 'High' for 1 minute. Release the pressure naturally for 7 minutes. Stir. Sauté for 1 minute while stirring to thicken sauce.

Use sauce on top of desserts or as a side dish. Refrigerate any leftovers in a sealed container.

Rice Pudding

Ingredients
Serves: 2-3

1 cup Arborio rice
¾ cup raisins (optional)
1 ½ cups water
½ tsp vanilla extract
¼ tsp salt
2 eggs
2 cups milk
½ cup sugar substitute (Splenda or Truvia)

Method:

Add the water, rice and salt to the Instant Pot and cook on 'High' for 3 minutes. Release the pressure naturally for 10 minutes, and then quickly release any remaining pressure.

Now add just 1 ½ cups of the milk to the pot, along with all of the sugar substitute. Stir well. Set to one side.

Take a mixing bowl and in it add the eggs, vanilla, and remaining milk. Whisk and then strain this mixture through a fine strainer. Add into the Pot. Press 'Sauté' and stir until the mix is starting to boil. Remove the pot from the cooker and add the raisins. Stir. Allow to cool slightly and serve.

Note: I often put the previous cranberry compote recipe as a garnish for the rice pudding.

Blueberry Bundt Cake

Serves- 6
Ingredients:

5 eggs
1/4 cup sugar substitute (Splenda or Truvia)
2 TBS butter, melted
3/4 cup ricotta cheese
3/4 cup vanilla Greek yogurt
2 tsp vanilla extract
2 tsp baking powder
1 TBSP orange rind (finely grated)

1 cup whole wheat pastry flour
1/2 tsp salt
¾ cup blueberries (fresh or frozen)
1 cup water

Method

Beat together the eggs and sugar substitute until smooth. Add the melted butter, vanilla, ricotta cheese, and Greek yogurt.

In a separate bowl, whisk together the flour, salt, and baking powder. Combine with the liquid mixture. Gently fold in the blueberries and grated orange. Pour into a prepared 6 section Bundt pan.

Place 1 cup of water in the Instant Pot reservoir. Add a trivet and place the Bundt pan on the trivet. Place the lid on and seal pressure knob. Cook on "high" for 25 minutes. Naturally release pressure for 10 minutes. Let cool and then serve.

Evelyn Carmichael

CHAPTER 7. HINTS AND TIPS

Quick Tips

- An Instant Pot operates at 242degrees F whereas a Pressure Cooker operates at 250 degrees F. If you are trying a recipe for a Pressure Cooker in your Instant Pot, make sure you add slightly more cooking time.
- The Instant Pot is extremely easy to clean! Washing the cooking pot and wiping down the housing unit is all you need for a normal clean. Deep cleaning is a bit more involved, but only needs to be done every once in a while.
- Do not try to can goods in the Instant Pot.
- You can cook food directly from its frozen state but need to add some time (for example 14 minutes for fresh chicken/ 20 for frozen).
- Make sure you read your Instant Pot instructions about coming up to pressure and releasing pressure. Naturally releasing pressure can take some time and can make a big difference proper food temperature if you do not familiarize yourself with this function.
- Some people choose not to make pasta in their Instant Pot, stating that it can clog the valves. I haven't had this issue, but I do often add a TBS of olive oil to the water which helps with the pasta from sticking as well.

How to store your meals

Here's a little tip for you. If you cook your meals in batches, you'll find the Instant Pot is ideal. I often double or triple most recipes. Simply make the meal in question, divide it into tubs, pots, or bags and allow the meal to cool. Once cooled, store it in your freezer until you're ready to eat it. All you need to do then is remove it from the freezer, and defrost in the fridge or microwave. Heat and enjoy!

Foods that can help

Below you will find a little information about foods that can help to maintain your sugar levels. Feel free to add to the provided recipes or your own Instant Pot recipes.

Nuts and seeds
Although some nuts are thought to be high in fat, in reality they are quite good for us. This is because the can contain omega 3 oils which are good for our joints, and our heart. Nuts and seeds can also keep us feeling satisfied for a little longer too.

Berries
You should ideally eat a few berries each day, this is because they contain slow-releasing sugars.

Ginger
Ginger is one of the healthiest foods that you can eat. An anti-inflammatory, anti-carcinogenic and digestive aid, it will help to keep your sugar levels stable too.

Garlic
Garlic is great for your heart, it can help to reduce inflammation, and it also works as an anti-viral, anti-bacterial, anti-carcinogenic, and anti-fungal. It also tastes good, and can help you to feel a little fuller for longer.

This book contains some tasty recipes that can help you to keep your sugar level stable. I know that you may be cooking for yourself for the first time, and this may be a little nerve-wracking, but chances are you'll enjoy it. Start off slowly, and don't expect to be the best cook around. We all had to start somewhere, and now it's your time to. Get used to eating homemade meals that are delicious, and healthy, without being full of unwanted sugars that can make you feel ill. Learn how to control your diabetes, just as I have, and learn to create tasty dishes in your Instant Pot, leaving you a lot less likely to reach for those sugary snacks. Make a difference to your health today, and use your Instant Pot to your advantage.

Experimenting with the recipes

When it comes to following the recipes in this book, please don't think that you have to stick to them. As with any dish, you know what works well to keep your blood sugar stable and how to play around with recipes. You should feel free to change a few of the ingredients if you wish, or even add a little something extra to the meal.   An Instant Pot really is a lot like a pressure cooker, but can do so much more to reduce the need to dirty up a ton of other pots and pans. The point of cooking homemade meals is to have fun, provide unparalleled nutrition and taste, add your own spin, and be proud of the food you are serving to you and your family.   Enjoy!

Read on for an excerpt of Evelyn Carmichael's book *The Essential Handbook to Reversing Prediabetes and Diabetes*, now on Amazon.

The Essential Handbook to
Diabetic Instant Pot Cooking

Evelyn Carmichael

THE ESSENTIAL HANDBOOK TO REVERSING PREDIABETES AND DIABETES

MEAL PLANS AND RECIPES TO REDUCE YOUR BLOOD SUGAR LEVELS AND ELIMINATE DIABETES AND PREDIABETES

By
EVELYN CARMICHAEL

Copyright © 2017

Evelyn Carmichael

INTRODUCTION

Millions of people throughout the globe suffer from
Prediabetes and Diabetes, but not everyone is aware that
they can reverse it simply by changing the way they eat. If
you suffer from Prediabetes or Diabetes, diet, exercise, and
your overall weight can play a significant part in your
blood sugar level. This book concentrates on specific foods
and how you choose food that will be beneficial in reducing
and even reversing your diagnosis. For those that have not
been diagnosed, but have a family history of Diabetes or
have seen their blood sugar levels inching up as the years
go by, following this meal plan and tips could keep you
from reaching a Diabetes diagnosis.

The recipes contained within this book are there to help you
change your health and ultimately your life for the better.
Start making yourself healthier today by using the meal
plans and recipes in this book. Learn how to swap healthy
ingredients to your own favorite recipes. In just a few
weeks, you will be able to see changes to your blood sugar
level that can reduce your need of medication or even
reverse the diagnosis of Prediabetes or Diabetes all
together. Plus, with your blood sugar levels stabilizing,
you will feel better than you have

Evelyn Carmichael

CHAPTER 1. WHAT IS DIABETES?

Millions of people around the world have been diagnosed with Prediabetes and Diabetes. In fact, approximately 12% of Americans over 20 years of age have been diagnosed with Diabetes. This disorder occurs when the food you eat is not properly processed as energy. Most of the food we eat is turned into glucose, or sugar, which our body uses for energy. The pancreas, an organ that lies near the stomach, makes a hormone called insulin to help glucose get into the cells of our bodies. When you have Diabetes, your body either doesn't make enough insulin or can't use its own insulin as well as it should. This causes sugars to build up in your blood.

Diabetes can cause serious health complications including heart disease, nerve damage, kidney failure, strokes, dental disease, eye problems, and lower-extremity amputations. Diabetes is the seventh leading cause of death in the United States.

According to the Center for Disease Control and Prevention, these are some of the symptoms of Diabetes: Frequent urination, excessive thirst, unexplained weight loss, extreme hunger, sudden vision changes, tingling or numbness in hands or feet, feeling very tired much of the time, very dry skin, sores that are slow to heal, and more infections than usual.

There are three main types of Diabetes:

TYPE 1 DIABETES

If you have type 1 Diabetes, your body does not make insulin and in fact destroys the cells in your pancreas that makes the insulin. Type 1 Diabetes is usually diagnosed in children and young adults, although it can appear at any age. People with type 1 Diabetes need to take insulin every day to stay alive.

GESTATIONAL DIABETES

Gestational Diabetes develops in some women when they are pregnant. It is estimated to effect 2-5% of all pregnancies. Most of the time, this type of Diabetes goes away after the baby is born. However, if you've had Gestational Diabetes, you have a greater chance of developing type 2 Diabetes later in life.

TYPE 2 DIABETES

If you have Type 2 Diabetes, your body does not make or use insulin well. You can develop type 2 Diabetes at any age, even during childhood. However, this type of Diabetes occurs most often in middle-aged and older people. There is a correlation between being overweight and a genetic history with Type 2 Diabetes. Type 2 is the most common type of

Diabetes with over 95% of all Diabetes diagnosis being in this category.

Prediabetes

Prediabetes, also known as Borderline Diabetic, is a growing disorder. Prediabetes means that your blood sugar level is higher than normal but not yet high enough to be Type 2 Diabetes. Without lifestyle changes, people with Prediabetes are very likely to progress to Type 2 Diabetes. According to the Center for Disease Control and Prevention, more than 86 million Americans have Prediabetes which is 1 out of 3 Americans. To make matters worse, 9 out of 10 people do not even know they have it.

This book will focus on Type 2 Diabetes and Prediabetes and the ability that food has to reverse or considerably change the severity of these conditions. If you have been diagnosed with Prediabetes or Diabetes, please make sure you discuss with your doctor any planned changes to your diet.

To find out more about Reversing Diabetes please visit https://www.amazon.com/Essential-Handbook-Reversing-Prediabetes-Diabetes-ebook/dp/B06WD7FSN3/.

Evelyn Carmichael

ABOUT THE AUTHOR

Evelyn Carmichael

Evelyn was in the world of corporate finance before switching her life path after a successful battle with breast cancer. She is a personal life coach, fitness guru, and healthy lifestyle advocate.

Find out more on Facebook or at https://www.amazon.com/Evelyn-Carmichael/e/B01MQYHZLC

Evelyn Carmichael

OTHER BOOKS BY EVELYN CARMICHAEL

Evelyn is the author of the Essential Handbook Series. Her titles include the following:

The Essential Handbook to Superfood Smoothies

The Essential Handbook to Hashimoto's

The Essential Handbook to Hygge

The Essential Handbook to Avocados The Superfood that Reduce Inflammation and lowers blood sugar, blood pressure, and your cholesterol

The Essential Handbook to Reversing Prediabetes and Diabetes: Meal Plans and Recipes to Reduce Your Blood Sugar Levels and Eliminate Diabetes and Prediabetes

The Essential Handbook to Turmeric and Ginger: The Anti-Inflammatory Duo that will Change your Life

The Essential Handbook to Coconut Oil: Tips, Recipes, and How to use for weight loss and in your daily life

Evelyn Carmichael

The Essential Handbook to Apple Cider Vinegar: Tips and Recipes for Weight Loss and Improving your Health, Beauty, & Home

The Art of Keeping Goals

The Essential Handbook for Choosing the Right Diet: A Guide to the Most Popular Diets and if They are Right for You

The Essential Handbook to Natural Living
The Essential Handbook to Essential Oils: Tips and Recipes for Weight Loss, Stress Relief, and Pain Management

Knee Supports: Uses, Exercises, and Benefits

*The Essential Handbook to
Diabetic Instant Pot Cooking*

Evelyn Carmichael

AUTHOR NOTE

If you enjoyed this book, found it useful or otherwise
then I'd really appreciate it if you would post a short
review on Amazon. I do read all the reviews personally
so that I can continually write what people are
wanting.
Thanks for your support!

Evelyn Carmichael

49841198R00056

Made in the USA
Lexington, KY
23 August 2019